Jean B. Dureau

The Sugar Question as It Affects the Consumer

Jean B. Dureau

The Sugar Question as It Affects the Consumer

ISBN/EAN: 9783337891558

Printed in Europe, USA, Canada, Australia, Japan

Cover: Foto ©Andreas Hilbeck / pixelio.de

More available books at **www.hansebooks.com**

THE

SUGAR QUESTION

AS IT AFFECTS

THE CONSUMER.

BY

M. B. DUREAU.

"IN INDICIS STAGNIS NASCI ARUNDINES CALAMIQUE DICUNTUR, EX QUORUM RADICIBUS EXPRESSUM SUAVISSIMUM SUCCUM DIBUNT."—*Isidorus.*

EDITED BY JOSEPH TRAVERS & SONS.

LONDON:

LONGMAN, GREEN, LONGMAN, ROBERTS, & GREEN.

1864.

LONDON :

PRINTED BY M. S. RICKERBY, BELL COURT,

4A, WALBROOK. E.C.

PREFACE.

WE have obtained the Author's permission to publish the following translation, the original of which appeared last year in Paris ; and if it prove the means of calling the attention of but a few of those Englishmen who understand the subject, to that original, we shall be satisfied with the result of an effort which we feel might be happier.

The existence of a large agricultural Sugar-growing interest in France must be borne in mind while reading M. Dureau's remarks. It is the identity of interest of this and the consuming class in France, and their antagonism to the class corresponding to our English refiners, that M. Dureau insists upon, and, as we think, establishes.

The French beet-root Sugar-maker is represented on our side of the Channel by the foreign planter, and whilst M. Dureau advocates the cause of the French consumer and grower, he advocates the cause of the Sugar-growers and consumers of all the world.

In spite of the veil thrown by translation over the style of the original, the greatness of the subject, the facts and figures it discloses, and the ability with which the author has handled the whole, justify us in hoping that it will find many readers.

J. TRAVERS & SONS.

19, SWITHIN'S LANE, LONDON.

" *Indica non magna minus arbore crescit arundo.*
Illius e lentis premitur radicibus humor,
Dulcia cui nequeant sucro contendere mella."

VARRONIS ATACINI FRAGMENTA.

ONE of the most difficult questions in the political economy of the present day—one of those questions which have for a long time required a solution, and which, by the numerous interests they involve, can seldom be dispassionately discussed—again presses itself upon the attention of Government, and of the public ; neither of which can remain indifferent to it. By these words we have sufficiently characterized the Sugar question.

But, let it be well understood, we are not going to enter into a retrospective controversy on this perpetually-recurring and vexatious question. We have no desire to grope our way in the dark path which it has formed during the last twenty years, (so distinguished for their civilization,) which have solved the problems of steam navigation, railways, and electric telegraphs, but have not yet been able to solve that of Sugar.

A solution of the question, however, is demanded : the interests of the grower, the consumer, and the

B 2

Exchequer require it, and the head of the State himself invites it by the expression of the enlightened views which his liberal mind entertains on this important subject.

Let us, then, endeavour to discover this solution, or at least the elements of it, that it may be conclusive at last, and bear the lasting stamp of union between the past and the future.

.

I.

What was the Sugar question in times gone by?

May we be spared from having to write its history; it would fill a volume which we should not have time to write, or the public courage to read. A few words will suffice to explain it; and to that end we cannot do better than call to remembrance the Roman orator who represented the governing power as a ball tossed alternately from one party to another. Is not this in a measure the history of the unhappy Sugar question; and might we not in a similar manner compare it to a ball tossed to and fro between the refiner and the beet-root grower; between the colonial and the foreign grower, bandied alternately from one to the other without ever being allowed to settle, or fall outside the fatal circle of players to whom it has so long been confined?

But it may be said, is not this a dispute between refiners and producers, between the colonies and the mother
country, between maritime and agricultural interests,
between cane and beet-root? What possible interest
can the public take in this tedious discussion? Putting
justice and equity on one side, it interests them greatly.

Let us suppose a dispute arising among corn-grow-
ers, millers, and bakers. Would not that disturbance
interest us? Supposing the farmers, graziers, and
butchers were to coalesce in order to raise the price of
meat. Should not such a coalition be put down for the
public good? Again, if the wine trade were shackled
by any cause whatever, so that this national and salu-
tary beverage could only reach the consumer under such
conditions as to stop or restrict considerably its consumption, should we not be all interested in the
suggestion of a remedy for such a state of things? or
if a company assumed the exclusive right of extracting
salt from sea-water, what would be said of such a
monopoly?

We say, then, that Sugar possesses the same title to
our interest, though not perhaps in the same degree, as
the necessary commodities we have just named; for this
condiment, the sources of which industry has so largely

increased, constitutes now an indispensable part of our food, beneficial alike to the poor and the affluent, to the workman and the idler, to the manual and the intellectual labourer, in the camp and the work-shop, in short it is useful to all ; humanity is interested in its general use, in its extension among all classes, and in its diffusion like any other of God's blessings on those inferior classes of society which have an equal right, with us, to air, water, and light, and should have an equal share, so far as their means may allow, in the daily commodities created by social industry, partaking of Sugar as they do of bread, of meat, of wine, and of salt.

The Sugar question is, therefore, of great importance to the public ; and more than this, the interest of the consumer should be first considered.

III.

It will not be sufficient to call the attention of the public to the question of principle ; we must besides enlighten it as to facts, explaining, in a few words, whence this new conflict, and what is the most recent cause of the agitation it has excited, not only in our own ports, but in our colonies, and in Sugar-growing districts.

We know that the imperial letter of January the 5th, 1860, has inaugurated in France a new system of political economy, based on the principle of Free

Trade, a system which has been successively applied to our agriculture and principal manufacturing interests. Sugar could not escape these modifications or remain undisturbed by this movement, which first affected it by the law of May 23rd, 1860, putting in practice the ideas long entertained on the reduction of the tax, suppressing the standards, and restoring freedom to native production by the *abonnement* * (compounded tax).

A decree of the 16th January, 1861, suppressed the extra-duty of three francs imposed on the foreign Sugars imported in French bottoms. Pursuing its reforms, the Government, by a second decree of the 24th June, 1861, allowed the drawback on foreign Sugars imported in foreign bottoms. By another decree of the 10th June, 1862, Havana Sugars imported in Spanish bottoms were no longer admitted to the drawback, without paying the navigation extra-duty. And, lastly, in consequence of certain financial exigencies, explained in M. Fould's report, the duty on Sugars was increased 12 francs per 100 kilogrammes, beginning from the 1st July, 1862. Such are the acts which characterise the last phase of the Sugar question, and which are the only ones we have to examine, since they alone have caused the controversy that has just arisen.

The law of the 23rd May, 1860, by the reduction of the tax, by the suppression of the ancient standards, and by the *abonnement* (compounded tax), necessarily favoured the interests of the consumer.

---

* See Note, page 67.

The decrees of the 16th January and the 24th June, 1861, no doubt had Free Trade in view.

The increased duty was a financial regulation of a purely temporary character.

The law of May 23rd, 1860, excited no serious opposition, as it favoured at the same time the interests of the grower, the consumer, and the refiner himself. The reason of this we shall explain hereafter. Not so with the decrees that followed, the effect of which was to open our ports to foreign Sugars, to encourage exportation by means of a disguised premium, to expose the practical inconsistency of our Sugar legislation, and, lastly, to bring the price of Sugar to a level far below that of the worst times, and of which even the year 1848 did not offer so bad an example. Hence the numerous complaints from our colonies, our ports, our beet Sugar manufactories, and all that are directly or indirectly interested in the manufacture or commerce of Sugar,— some demanding the re-establishment of the extra-duty on foreign Sugars; others, that the faculty of exportation should be limited to Sugars imported in French bottoms : the former would have the drawback limited to refined home-grown Sugar ; the latter considered that they ought to oppose it,—or, at least, if they allowed such Sugars to be exported, it should be with the re-establishment of the standards. And thus it is we find practical results denied, and ourselves again engaged in the controversy on the Sugar question.

IV.

All things affected by the law of progress, are represented by advanced or retrograde opinions; and the
excitement of the existing contest between the systems
of protection and free trade proves how passionately
we can enter into the discussion of industrial or commercial affairs. No one, therefore, will be surprised at
our affirming that the Sugar question has "its Tories "*
in the present day. It is true this party is more
distinguished by its numbers than by its consistency,
but it is nevertheless dangerous through its tradi-
tional influence and the experience it is supposed to
possess. Composed almost entirely of seaport merchants, cosmopolitan ship-owners, refiners, slow-minded
retired manufacturers, and a few middle-men, it forms
a sort of army of Coblentz, which has for its avowed
aim the reversal of all new regulations about Sugar,
the first blows of which are to be directed against
the law of May 23rd, 1860,—that advanced outpost
in the progress of the Sugar trade.

It must be known that this very law of 1860, now
about to be attacked, is the first truly liberal legislative act respecting Sugar; that it is the necessary
consequence of the Emperor's political programme; and
that it is, in a word, the most recent sign of progress

---

* We use the term "Tories" as the nearest equivalent to the well-known
phrase "*ses anciens partis.*" No literal rendering of the term, such as
"old or former parties," would convey to the English reader its exact
meaning.—ED.

resulting from our commercial reforms. The law of May 23rd, 1860, besides reducing the tax on Sugar, has introduced in our Sugar legislation the fruitful and equitable principle of equal duties. By the *abonnement*, it has emancipated the native manufacturer from the troubles and vexations of the excise ; by suppressing the ancient standards, it has opened the door to a progress, which has shown itself in a general improvement of beet Sugar manufacture, by the introduction of richer Sugars to the French market so much desired by the foreign refiners, and the erection of a number of magnificent factories both in France and our colonies, which the reactionists would shut up or render useless.

Energetically opposed in the beginning by all the independent refiners, and a number of prejudiced beet Sugar manufacturers, it has, nevertheless, failed to produce that revolution with which we were threatened, and is a proof that a union of interests is better than opposition. Where are the refineries it has closed ? Where are the manufacturers it has exclusively benefited ? And who are those who can conscientiously complain of it ? Never has the refinery of Sugar been more prosperous ; never have finer materials been brought to the refiners ; and never has greater progress been made in the beet manufacture. You complain of a legislation already adopted in a portion of Europe, and which England herself, intent on its application, is now carefully studying, so favourably does it promise even to her consumption,—the greatest in the world ! You complain of unity, simplicity, and progress ! Truly, you belong to the ancient party of abuse, of monopoly, and of privilege. You are the party who have retained, for twenty years, a question of political economy without being able to solve it; a question which you would fain attempt to perpetuate. We have called you the Sugar army of Coblentz: modern comedy would give you another name; ask it rather of M. Victorien Sardou.*

V.

One of the greatest proofs of progress in modern times is the considerable and incessant reduction of price in the objects of large consumption; a reduction which is owing to two principal causes,—the general application of machinery, and the progressive liberty of commercial transactions. If it has required a succession of great mechanical and chemical improvements to bring within our reach, and in great abundance, manufactured commodities such as iron, cotton, paper, soap, and many other products too numerous to name, it has also required a succession of commercial reforms which are progressing at the present day. With regard to Sugar, it would certainly be as little known now as it was in the eighteenth century, and even the beginning of the nineteenth, were it not for the double progress above mentioned; its history, in this respect, does not differ from any other products which are affected by the joint influences of machinery and legis-

---

* See Note, page 68.

lation, and it is thus, by the happy concurrence of industrial and economical agencies, that material comfort has been raised to its present height. Do you wish to make much Sugar? Do you wish to sell it cheap? If so, you must have as liberal and as perfect a legislation of its kind as are your own manufacturing instruments. Do you suppose refined Sugar could be sold in France for the price we now pay, were it not, first, for the power and perfection of our machinery, and subsequently for the law of May 23rd, 1860? These two terms, progress and legislation, are inseparable; whence the practical conclusion that legislation ought to pay the greatest attention to the progress of industry, and to comply with its rational development.

Certain savage nations flatten the heads of their children between two boards, thinking to make them more beautiful by the process; this resembles the political economy of the past. How many monopolies, privileges, restrictions, prohibitions, absurdities are there on account of Sugar, which have lasted for two centuries, and which they still think is not long enough! Opponents of a single duty, and to all the improvements comprised in the manufacture of Sugar, you have a pedigree which dates from *Father Labat.*[*] It was you who, in 1682, imposed an extra-duty on those white Sugars which were then manufactured to advantage in our West Indian colonies. It was you who, in 1684, obtained an order of the Privy Council forbidding the erection of new refineries in those islands. We recognise your signature to the

---

[*] See Note, page 69.

decree of 1791, which inaugurated in France the æra of classification, and reduced the fabrication of colonial Sugar to the condition in which it was found by M. Peligot, in 1842. We see it again in the restrictive laws of 1814, '16, and '20, always striking at white Sugar, in the interest of the refiners. It was you who made tha law of the 26th April, 1833, which established so enormous a fiscal distinction between raw and white Sugars. It was you who made the two standards of the law of 1843, a restraint vainly employed against that progress which the illustrious prisoner of Ham then defended, in the following words :—

"It is evident that the obligation imposed on the "planter, to send nothing but impure Sugars to France, "in order to preserve for that produce its greatest por- "table weight, is a law only fit for barbarians." *

We find you again, in 1846 and 1851, persecuting the home manufacture (*beet-root*) with your impotent rancour, strangling it by the excise duty, and by restrictions on the power of refining in manufactories, and we recognise you in everything that could arrest its progress or development. Condemned by you for the very important help it afforded national agri- culture, you have by your joint efforts laid it on the bed of Procrustes, saying, "You shall increase no "longer, you shall go no further!" But time has done justice to your opposition and your rancour. Kept in check by the law of May 23rd, 1860, (a law - so liberal, so eminently favourable to progress, and the

---

* "Analysis of the Sugar Question," by Prince Napoleon Bonaparte. 1842.

fruits of which have been gathered, as we have before
shown,) you rise again before us in 1864, and, as we
know you of old, we have a right to say, "What is it
you want now?"

VI.

You want to arrest the development of our great and
admirable manufacture of beet-root Sugar, less on account of its production, which has outstepped you, than
for that of the progress it is daily making, and
which you presume to stem. The seed deposited in
the national soil, by the first Napoleon, half a century
ago, has borne fruit ; the tree has grown ; it has thrown
out innumerable roots ; it affords you shade ; and you
want to destroy its branches! Yet what industry
is more noble, more useful ; and what are all your
petty interests compared to it! "Respect me," said
the illustrious writer we have just quoted, twenty years
ago, "for I enrich the land, and fertilise soils, which,
"without me, would remain uncultivated ; I employ
"hands which, without me, would remain idle."
Respect it, could we add in our turn, if we might
be allowed to follow the thought of so high an
authority, for it has justified, not to say surpassed,
all the hopes founded on it. At once manufacturing and agricultural, it is one of the bases of national
prosperity, one of the conditions necessary to the
existence of a part of our rural population, and the

hopes of our improved agriculture. By its double character, by its vitality, which nothing can impair, by the productive forces it developes on all sides, it has acquired the highest sympathies; and this "daughter of the Empire" has become the spoiled child of that science, which devotes a constant attention to it. Closely connected with the social economy of our richest and most fertile countries, its prosperity is their prosperity, its futurity their futurity.

But this industry is so natural to the soil, and is gifted with such a power of expansion, that it has easily penetrated innumerable localities, where it quickens agriculture, which in return re-acts upon it. Thus wherever it reaches, wherever it stops, wherever it takes root, the beneficial influence of its capital, its salaries, and its stirring activity is immediately felt. Its action is no longer limited to one or two districts. It may extend to almost every one ; and this is one of the causes of the continual increase in its production, which has been doubled every ten years. It is now 170 millions kilos. ; and in that proportion it may be 500 millions kilos. in the year 1900. A thousand manufactories of beet Sugar will then cover that happy and prosperous France, which, blessed with the riches acquired by a progress to which our generation will have mainly contributed, will then look back with pride on that period, teeming with the richest discoveries, when the members of the Academy, forming a deputation, presented their illustrious colleague, the first Emperor, with the first loaf made of beet-root Sugar !

What progress since then have we made ? Why, from a return of 1 or 2 per cent., we arrive at a produce of 6 per cent., which may, perhaps, ultimately reach 7 or 8 per cent.; from a manufacturing price of 4 or 5 francs per pound, we may descend to 25 or 30 centimes, for this is the price beet-root Sugar may come to, if not impeded in its progress! Is not this a wonderful result, to have been obtained in so short a time? We do not here speak of any of those sources of production to be met with in the early ages, such, for example, as metals; but an industry of our own times, of which some of our present manufacturers may have seen the beginning. Its opponents will not fail to rejoin that this result is owing to the protection it enjoyed at first. And when was that? Have we not all worn leading-strings, and is not maternity, in her tender care, a protection? And who amongst those who make this reproach have not also been under the yoke of that protection which they disdain for others, but which they accept for themselves? However, no branch of industry is less protected and more completely left to its own resources,—resources which we may hope will not be found wanting in its future career.

It is now free, though some would impede its progress; it is strong, though some would reduce its power; it is gradually harmonizing with the future, though some would gladly drive it back to the past; as if its liberty, its strength, and its progress, were not the logical consequence of the general progress of industry, and with which progress it is closely bound up. .

With regard to authenticated facts, we may say that the constant tendency of the native Sugar-manufacture has always been, not only to increase its per-centage, by making more and more Sugar, with the same quantity of beet-root, but also to make it whiter, richer, purer, more fit for immediate consumption, and enabling it to be refined with less trouble and expense. It is at this time, when the goal is nearly attained, that a league of opposing interests endeavours to deny this immense progress, and strives by every effort to cramp its action in proposing we know not what system, by which the producer, placed at the bottom of the ladder, can only ascend its successive steps by help of the refiner placed at the summit. That is a compact, however, to which native industry cannot submit any more than our colonial interests, which, on their part, aspire to self-government, and require perfect liberty.

VII.

The true principle of taxation is, that it should be established in such a manner as to be least felt by those who have to bear its burden. Antiquity represents Camilla gliding over a field of corn without bending a stem ; thus lightly should the weight of taxation fall on all that pertains to industry. But what ought we to think of a legislative measure which for nearly two centuries has weighed on the producer, presenting an insurmountable obstruction to all progress ? This obstruction is the standard scale ; it is the graduated tax which, to this

c

day, even among beet-manufacturers, finds a few supporters, as if it were not an old worn-out war contri-
vance, only to be compared to the catapults and battle-
axes of middle ages. "Give us back our standards,"
say they; rather should they say, "Give us back our
"chains." Is that, then, the price to be paid for
the admission of native Sugar to the drawback, which,
after all, is a common right, and should be granted
unconditionally? Oh! if such be the case, and
our protestations could reach the head of the
State, we would say :—" Sire, our native beet-root
" Sugar has experienced many trials already ; pray
" spare it this one; and, if the re-establishment
" of the scale must precede the right of exportation,
" we will give up at once that privilege, rather than
" return to a system of classification so contrary to
" our interests, and which has been condemned by
" yourself, Sire, without appeal."

In the past, the history of the extra-duty is one of
the most curious chapters to be added to the account
of privileges, abuses, and monopolies. It had no other
object than to supply the merchant service with a
greater amount of freight, and to keep up the privileged refineries of the metropolis ; and, even as late
as 1843, we meet with those despicable arguments,
which arrested during two centuries the free expansion
of our Sugar-manufactory.

At present,—and that present has already had
twenty years' duration,—the extra-duty is condemned
the moment it is proved that Sugar, as it exists in
the cane and in the beet-root, is white, and that it

may be extracted white, and in larger quantities when
no portion of it is destroyed by an imperfect process,
or by imperfect instruments.* Experience and science
condemn the system of standards ; but they would
revive it in the name of political economy, which
equally condemns it ; as if what is absurd for the one
is not equally so for the other ; as if true science had
two weights and measures ; as if reason and logic
were not always in harmony. Thus chemistry says
to the manufacturers, " Make white Sugar ;" whilst
political economy says, " Make brown Sugar."
Such is, in short, the point of our opponents' argument.

There is but one misfortune ; it comes too late,
and is contradicted by the tendency of almost all
modern legislation on Sugar. The United States,
which, after England, have the largest consumption
of Sugar in the world, are under the regulations of the
Morril Tariff, which admits of only two classes—
refined and non-refined Sugar, and establishes only two
duties. Holland, with considerable colonial interests,
and a great refining interest, has only two duties,
one on raw Sugar, without distinction of colour, the
other on refined. Belgium, with a tolerably complicated legislation, has but two duties. The Zollverein
has but two duties. Russia has several duties, according to the importation being effected by land or water,
but with only two great classifications—raw and
refined. Spain has highly protective duties with
regard to its shipping and colonies ; but its customs
still follow the same principle—raw and refined.

---

* See Note—Governor Barkly's Report, p. 70.

The colony of the Cape has but two duties. Lastly, the young colony of Australia, a nation which belongs to the future, has gone further than any in the path of progress, and has but one duty, whether the Sugars are refined or not, and which has not prevented the establishment of a large refinery in Melbourne. France, therefore, has not engaged alone in the suppression of these ancient standards ; and if she be mistaken, it is in a good and numerous company.

England alone has retained the graduated scale to the present day, and recognises, as we know, four standards, and even six, counting Molasses and cane juice. Mr. Gladstone's tariff of 1854 establishes the scale of duties on the following basis :—

	£	s.	d.
		cwt.	
Candy, brown or white. Refined Sugar, or Sugar rendered by any process equal in quality thereto	0	18	4
White clayed Sugar, or Sugar rendered by any process equal in quality to white clayed, not being refined, or equal in quality to refined	0	16	0
Yellow Muscovado and brown clayed Sugar, or Sugar rendered by any process equal in quality to yellow Muscovado or brown clayed, and not equal to white clayed	0	13	10
Brown Muscovado, or any other Sugar, not being equal in quality to yellow Muscovado or brown clayed Sugar	0	12	8
Cane Juice	0	10	4
Molasses	0	5	0

A tariff based on such subtle distinctions must in the application raise the greatest difficulties, and annihilate the value of that improved process of fabrication which the English Government, by fixing a single duty on free and slave-grown Sugars, had induced the colonies to adopt. How is it possible to distinguish the slight difference which separates an inferior quality from the one just above it ? Thus, a Sugar at

12s. 8d. will be taxed at 13s. 10d. by the Custom-house officer, whilst the purchaser will offer a price based on the lower duty. From 13s. 10d. the duty rises suddenly to 16s., upon Sugar which may be identically the same, or which differs only by an imperceptible shade, dependent on a foggy or clear sky, a damp or dry atmosphere, or even on the power of vision, and perhaps on the temper of the assessor at the Custom-house. Therefore, it was not without reason that a gentleman interested in the Sugar question remarked, in Mr. Gladstone's presence, that it would be requisite to supply the Custom-house officers entrusted with the application of this wonderful tariff " with *standard eyes*." And it is a legislation sanctioning such absurdities as these, and which existed in France previous to the law of May 23rd, 1860, that is now placed before us as a model.

Is it not also well known that all who are interested in the consumption of Sugar in England, the refiners excepted, are protesting against the legislation of 1854, and that a Select Committee has had lately to examine into the operation of this scale ? The result was a large volume,* which ought to be translated into French for its curious and important revelations. The Committee, it is true, does not report in favour of a single duty, though it advocates certain modifications. But it is not to these conclusions that we must look for the result of the inquiry ; it lies hidden in the minutes themselves—in the report of the

---

* " Report of the Select Committee on Sugar Duties," 1862.

sittings, in the depositions of the parties, and in the answers to the inquiries. Planters of the Mauritius, the East and West Indies, British Guiana, merchants of Mincing Lane, ship-owners, Sugar-brokers of every grade—all have agreed to condemn the differential tax, and to expose its evil effects, the greatest of which has been to establish the monopoly of about eighty refiners, who, from London, Liverpool, Southampton, Plymouth, Goole, Sheffield, Bristol, Glasgow, Dublin, and Greenock, command and farm the consumption of the United Kingdom, and have extended over the trade, for their own exclusive profit, an almost impenetrable net. Such are the results of that inquiry, and such the certain results of a legislation which similar interests in our own country invite us to admire, and, worse still, to imitate.

The French supporters of a differential tax have not hesitated to say that the slight duty of 12s. 8d., which corresponds to No. 9 of the Dutch mode of classification, was favourable to the consumption of the people, and that, in this respect, English legislation was more liberal than ours. But what they have not said, and what must be told, is this, that, out of the 500,000 tons which England at present consumes, there are not more than 10,000 tons of the favoured Sugar given directly to the public. And if we consider that the said Sugar at 12s. 8d. forms 60 per cent. of the quantity consumed, we shall have an idea of the monopoly of the refiners, who are quite willing to let the English people consume coarse Sugar, but only on condition that they shall supply it under the form of

Bastards and Pieces, and the last dregs of the refinery, including Molasses. But at least these products are clean, and free from those vile residues, those myriads of insects which colonial manufacturers are unable to separate, and which one of the honest manufacturers just alluded to, armed with his microscope, offered to reveal to the Committee, who, astounded at such a swarm of parasites in raw Sugar, were naturally led to conclude that the Jamaica planter, as well as the Mauritius and East Indian grower, was unable to send his produce to the consumer in a satisfactory condition without the manufacturing skill of the English refiner.—Admirable result' of the differential tax !*

VIII.

When the manufacturers of beet-root Sugar, at one of the last meetings convened in consequence of the late agitation, seemed to rally, partially at least, around that differential principle which might have been considered entirely abandoned since the law of May 23rd, 1860, they were evidently acting under the influence of the adversaries of white Sugar, produced by factories of the highest class, as if the question of a single standard, besides the refined, was not deeply interesting, more or less, to all producers.

---

* The sarcasm is just ; for without our differential duties, Sugars, in so impure a state as to contain acari, would hardly be manufactured, certainly never enter this kingdom. Their existence may be said to be due to the scale of duties.—ED.

But since they wanted a tariff similar to that on the other side of the channel, why did they not inquire a little more about what is taking place there ? They would have learned, perhaps, that since the application of that tariff, fine Sugars have ceased to be sent to England, to such a point, that the consumption of the 13s. 10d., corresponding to No. 14 Dutch number, which was 93 per cent. of the consumption of 1853, fell to 40 per cent. in 1861, whilst that of the 12s. 8d., or No. 9, increased from $2\frac{1}{2}$ per cent. to more than 55 per cent.* That might be found extremely profitable on the borders of the Clyde or the Thames, where refining has been carried on to a very great extent; but it is far different in the English Sugar colonies, where the Gladstone tariff has been the object of just complaints, and well-founded opposition, and where it has been found that the law has established a monstrous monopoly to the prejudice of the planter, who is taxed by a duty that rises in proportion to the greater care he has given to his manufacture and machinery. So that it may now be said on the banks of the Ganges, as well as in the West Indies, and in our own Sugar factories of the north, the dregs, the fermentations, the leavings of Molasses, *are good enough for England.*

It is impossible to doubt that the legislative enactments concerning a commodity in so much demand as Sugar must have a decided influence on the taste of the consumer. When the colony of

* From 1861 to 1863 the consumption of this class, the 12s. 8d., has still further increased to 60 per cent, showing how rapidly it is excluding every higher quality.— ED.

St. Domingo could manufacture white Sugar, when *rouler en blanc* was for a planter not only a speculation, but also a proud satisfaction, equal to that felt by the pessessor of a title, the metropolitan consumers were well satisfied with this powdered Sugar, which they would now proscribe, and the use of which, thanks to its low price, was continued, in respect to Bourbon, Manila, and Bengal Sugars, until the establishment of the standards ; until the triumph of the refiners who thus became the exclusive purveyors for French consumption. In England, the same causes have produced the same effects, with this difference, that the English people have remained faithful to the use of coarse Sugars, which are supplied to them under all forms by the refineries, instead of coming direct from the colonial planters as they used to do. It is worthy of remark, however, that the general taste is improving, and that the poor themselves are showing a decided dislike for the dark Sugars with which the English market is inundated. They want Sugar at 13s. 10d., and even at 16s., but, owing to the heavy duty, they are unable to obtain such. And thus it is that the English consumption is completely at the mercy of the refiners, from whom alone they can obtain the Sugar they prefer ; whilst, on the other hand, the planters of the West Indies, the Mauritius, and India, shackled by a barbarous legislation, and having no other outlet than the demands of the English refiner, take no pains to increase their produce or improve their implements, and are ten years behind the French planters.

The English colonies, in fact, are still content with the ancient *batterie*, the vacuums of Howard or Wetzell, and no establishment among those vast possessions which by themselves are sufficient to supply the consumption· of the whole world, is fit to be compared with the magnificent specimens of modern art to be seen in such small islands as Guadaloupe and Martinique. Consequently, the English Sugars are far below the ordinary quality to be met with in our French markets at the present day. Mauritius, it is true, manufactures much fine Sugar, but the planter finds no sale for it in England, where he only sends his syrup Sugars, whilst his finest produce goes to Australia or France, which, between them both, take half his crop.* In the Presidencies of Bengal and Madras, the coarse Sugar, bought of the ryots under the name of "jaggery," undergoes a semi-refining process, and might arrive perfectly pure in England, were it not for the scale of duties and the monopoly of the refiners.

In the West Indies there are many *vacuum pans*, and Jamaica produced a short time ago a quantity of very fine Sugar ; but there, as everywhere else, the planter is discouraged by the baneful effects of a tariff, concerning which the present condition of commerce, and of the English Sugar colonies, tells a sad tale ; and which is only supported by eighty refiners, whose success, however, is quite sufficient to raise the ambition of all those interested in the same trade in France.

Let our beet-manufacturers, then, learn from what is taking place in England, that the question of a single

---

* Exportations from Mauritius.—See Note, p. 72.

duty, and the maintenance of the law of May 23rd, 1860, so far as it regards standards, does not interest the manufacturers of white Sugar, and the more or -less fortunate possessors of highly-finished machinery only ; but white Sugar is a question for the consideration of our beet Sugar-manufacturers ; and if the principle of a fixed tax, which is at length admitted, is to benefit any branch of the Sugar-production, it is certainly that one whose produce cannot enter into direct consumption but after perfect purification, of which it would be most unjust to deny the means.

Whether the consumer or the refiner be considered, whether highly complicated machinery or common apparatus be employed, whether coarse or crystallized Sugar be produced, all our manufacturers have a common interest in improving the colour, in increasing the sweetening power of their Sugar, in giving up the old traditions of good fourth quality, and approaching closer and closer to the highest standard of colour and richness.

In order to make inferior and coarse Sugars you must have a coarse and inferior purifying apparatus, with a total disregard for all those processes which, in improving the quality, raise the per-centage of the Sugar produced, and increase the profit.*   A good manufac-

---

* It is a complete error to believe that a greater per-centage is obtained by making inferior Sugars; that might have been at a time when the whitening of Sugar was performed mechanically, whether in moulds or in turbines ; but it is not the same with the modern process, based on chemical action, and which purifies the syrup, so that the Sugar comes out white from the turbine.   Consequently, the manufacturers who produce the finest Sugar are those who get the highest per-centage, and who always obtain the greatest profit.

turer cannot make bad Sugars ; hence the natural
conclusion that the creation of several standards would
be an encouragement offered to bad manufacture, and
is the result directly aimed at in demanding the repeal
of a law having for its object the encouragement of
that which should be most respected, most favoured,
and made the best of.

The manufacturer who does not, or who cannot,
make any but coarse Sugars, deserves no kind of
protection ; for, when a bad manufacture is not the
consequence of a bad law, it is the result of bad
machinery, and we cannot admit that production under
such circumstances can be of any advantage to
the community. In any other circumstances what
should we think of legislative measures having for their
object the compensation of natural inequalities in the
means of production, such as a different soil, climate,
price of labour, fuel, or distance from the principal
markets, &c. It would evidently be a clear in-
fringement of the fundamental principles of com- .
mercial liberty, whose precise object is to supply
the greatest number with produce manufactured under
the most advantageous conditions. Is, then, the improved style of our manufacture the only one benefited by the law of May 23rd, 1860, and do we not
see that refining in general has never been more prosperous ? Thirty years ago, when good fourth quality
was at 160 francs the 100 kilogrammes, refined Sugar
was at 230 francs ; or a difference of 70 francs was
at that time found necessary, and even then the sale
was not effected without the addition of the envelope,

weighing 10 lb. per cwt., too well remembered by all
housekeepers of that day, and which raised this difference in reality to more than 90 francs. Now, when
good fourth quality is 100 francs duty-paid, loaf Sugar
is at most 130 francs, giving a difference of 30 francs,
or only one-third of what it was in 1830. Is not this
a very great advance, owing not only to greater skill
in the refiners, but principally to great improvements
in the manufacture of the first produce ; to the constant improvement of colour and strength in the raw
Sugars to be refined ? Grower, refiner, consumer, one
and all, have found out their advantages, and it is
precisely this legitimate satisfaction, given to interests
apparently opposed to each other, which characterises
the present age, and proves the goodness of the law.

Never, as we have before stated, has England
received a greater quantity of the worst Sugars ; and
never has France received richer or finer. France
has then become, since 1830, thanks to the suppression of the standards, the market for the first
Sugars, both in colour and quality. Let the standard
be re-established, and a contrary direction will be
taken, and France will receive those coarse Sugars we
had lost sight of, those Sugars, dripping with Molasses,
and losing as much as 10 per cent. on their voyage ;*
those Sugars, smelling of fermentation, smelling of
burnt matter, recking with the odour of bad manufacture ; those bottoms, those greasy, clayey Sugars, only

---

* In the evidence before the Select Committee of 1862, J. A. Tinne, Esq.,
one of the largest planters in the colony of Demerara, stated, that out of
26,956 cwt. of Sugar shipped by him from there in 1861, only 23,468 cwt.
were received in Liverpool, that is to say, a loss by drainage of 13 per cent. ! !
—ED.

fit for the refining pan, and which bear the indelible
stamp of routine, want of care, or low cunning ; for in
order to escape from a higher duty and remain below
what the English call the standard of colour, they will
do what evil they please, and mix lamp-black, dirt, or
ashes with the Sugar : such things have been, and will
be again ; and you call that encouraging manufactures ! For our part we cannot see what the nation
gains by such tricks and such frauds, which are not
suitable to the present times, and are repugnant to the
dignity of commerce and industry.

IX.

Certain inhabitants of the interior of Africa, exposed
to a constant equatorial heat, have heard of snow, but
have never seen it. With our lower classes, who are
the most numerous, it was for a long time the
same with regard to Sugar : they had heard of the
plant that produced it under a tropical sun, of the
negro slave who extracted it beneath the lash of the
driver, of the ship that crossed the ocean to bring it
to our ports along with precious spices ; they had heard
also of its beneficial properties, its sweet and grateful
flavour ; but they knew it was an article of luxury
reserved for the higher class, as the wines of Tokay or
Constantia are at the present day, and no one dreamed
of considering it as capable of being manufactured some
day in millions of tons, and becoming a commodity of

general consumption. The Romans, in regard to Sugar, were indebted to the industry of bees, and in the fourteenth century this commodity was worth 25 francs per lb. In consequence of the Continental blockade, Sugar, during the Empire, reached the price of 6 francs per lb., but after the Peace it returned to the same price as before the rupture with our colonial possessions, and remained from 1816 till 1830 between 2 and 3 francs per kilogramme for loaf Sugar. It has gradually fallen since then, till the progress of industry and judicious reforms in our legislation have reduced it to its present price.

The consumption of Sugar, under the Empire, was not more than 1 lb. per head in France ; whilst in England, then commanding the seas and holding all the colonial produce in the world, it was 16 lbs. English consumption then made an advance upon ours which it has preserved ever since. French consumption increased rapidly on the return of intercourse with our colonial and maritime possessions. But until 1846 it never exceeded 8 lbs. per head ; whilst in England, at the same period, it averaged 18 lbs.*
At the present time France consumes $6\frac{1}{2}$ lbs. less than England from 1801 to 1814, whilst the latter now consumes 34 lbs. per head more than France probably will in 1900 ; for in the consumption of Sugar, our neighbours are half a century in advance of us.

That French consumption is susceptible of considerable increase, although we do not make use of hot drinks as the English, is a supposition we

are led to make, if we consider how the 240 million
kilogrammes we consume annually are distributed
among the population. In England half the Sugar
used is consumed by the working classes; and we think
that the same estimate might be admitted for France.
In this calculation the share of the working classes
would be from 3 to 4 kilogrammes per head, whilst that
of the higher orders would reach 15 or 20 kilogrammes.

If we consider that Sugar is hardly ever an object
of luxury, but, on the contrary, a thing of primary
necessity, we see what a vast field remains open to
consumption, and what progress it might make if it
were encouraged both by reduction in the cost of
manufacture, and by legislative measures which favour
rational and cheap production.

A remarkable fact to be explained, undoubtedly by
the improvement of our habits and the constant
raising of salaries, is the greater disposition shown
by numerous classes for a better quality in their pro-
visions of primary necessity : we want better bread,
better meat, better drinks than before ; we want also
better and finer Sugar ; and this remark is, perhaps,
as applicable to England as to France. Who now eats
oatmeal or rye-bread ? Who would not prefer the
refined to the coarse Sugar with which our prede-
cessors were content, on account of the high price
of the former ? In England, as we have already
said, common Sugars can scarcely be sold, and it is
evident that the few who purchase them do so only
through poverty. Besides, low-priced Sugars are in
reality the dearest, on account of the Molasses and

impurities they contain. And what is the consequence ?
It is this : in consequence of the graduated tariff, there
are no longer to be found at the grocers the crushed
white, the clayed, or the fine raw moist Sugars,
which were to be had before 1854. The consumers
have, therefore, to apply to the refiners who supply
them, not with loaf Sugar, but with the dregs of the
factories, which are not equal to the Sugar imported
directly from the colonies, and yet necessarily command a higher price.

In general, English consumption is divided into two
classes—lumps and moist Sugar. It is the same in
Holland, Belgium, Germany, America : the one is the
Sugar of the rich, the other of the poor. In France,
it is said, "loaf Sugar is universally consumed, and
" no other ; they do not accept your theories, and
" have a sovereign contempt for your moist Sugar."
If so, how are we to explain the opposition you are
making against it ?   If it is an insignificant enemy, why
not leave it alone ?   If it is Utopian, why not allow it
to vanish like a dream ?   For our part, when we re-
member those magnificent products obtained directly
from the cane or the beet-root, which were seen at the
last universal Exhibition, and which have so justly
established our superiority in this branch of production,
we ask why we may not hope to triumph over all
obstacles, by the abundance and comparative cheapness
of this kind of product, which has all the qualities
of loaf Sugar, and can always be supplied at a lower
price.

More than this, a few statistical details will prove that

D

this particular manufacture (beet-root Sugar), which they want to check in its birth, has made, during the last three years, very considerable progress. The law of May 23rd, 1860, has established the existence, or transformation, of *forty-two* Sugar factories at home or abroad, capable of producing together 41 million kilogrammes of Sugar, 15 millions of which at least are fit for direct consumption ; the remainder attaining to No. 20, *i. e.*, to a standard nearly equal to refined Sugar. This marked progress, which answered so well the intentions of the legislature in 1860, took place as follows :—

1860. Four beet-root and two cane establishments, capable of producing together 7 million kilogrammes.

1861. Eight beet-root and nine cane, capable of producing 16 million kilos.

1862. Twelve beet-root and seven cane, capable of producing 18 million kilos.

We shall not surprise any one by saying that in the present year there is but a very small number of factories in course of erection or transformation. We know of but two in France, and four in the colonies.

But this is not all. The law of May 23rd, 1860, was not only a signal for establishing forty-two factories, which represent a seventh part of the whole of our Sugar-production, and whose condition would become deplorable, if the principle by virtue of which they had been established were abandoned. That law has also been the principal cause of a very considerable progress in all our home-manufactures ; for the lighter coloured Sugars being less taxed, and consequently more in demand among refiners, each manufacturer has arranged to make more of this sort.

The mean standard of beet-root Sugar at present has risen to No. 15, and the common qualities are nothing more than the production from inferior beet-root ; these the manufacturers can forward to England, since that country agrees to receive them, as it is her interest so to do ; whilst our refiners, on the contrary, find such advantage in working superior qualities, that we are still at a loss to comprehend the motives of those who wish to return to the old system of standards. The same remark applies to those beet-root Sugar-manufacturers who have ranged themselves under the retrograde banner of the Lille Committee. There must have been peculiar influences at work, to induce them to attack with such levity a law, in the application of which consists their best mode of opposing cane-produce, and of maintaining their home produce in that high position so necessary for its prosperity and influence.

We trust we have sufficiently proved that the question now before us is not new, and that each of the various interests engaged in the present contest has had its representative in the past. We can trace, from 1682 to the present day, the antagonism between loaf and moist Sugar, which were found by the reparatory law of May 23rd, 1860, in their usual hostile attitude. Is it, then, this law that has originated the process of refining in our home manufactories, which have been surrounded during the last

ten years with a network of rules and restrictions by
the subtilty of our independent refiners ? Did not the
manufacture of white Sugar exist in our colonies long
before France ever possessed suitable machinery, or
made white Sugar ? Has not Havannah always manufactured clayed Sugars, and British India semi-refined
qualities ? Has not Réunion manufactured during
thirty years Sugar fit for consumption ? Was not
Sugar refined at Martinique in the time of *Father
Labat ?* Have not the beet-root Sugar-manufacturers
themselves, scattered through forty or fifty of our
departments, tried a thousand unsuccessful experi-
ments for making white Sugar, which an increase
of knowledge would ultimately lead to a more satisfactory result ?

On the contrary, the question of white Sugar is
nothing new, any more than the opposition raised
against it, and which has given birth to the ingenious
war-contrivance called " the scale of standards." It has
actually been said that it caused the improvement of
the machinery, and that the interests of our engineers
themselves were at stake, forgetting that in 1842,
when Prince Louis Napoleon Bonaparte made himself
the disinterested advocate of white Sugar, there could
be no question concerning that kind of machinery,
which was not invented till ten years later. There
must certainly be in such an allegation, which
hardly deserves a reply, a marked calumny or a
serious error, and it must be a very bad cause which
requires such a means of defence. Besides, does the
English colonial grower, who has been for a long time

pleading the cause of white Sugar with a talent and
strength of argument, of which the Agricultural Board
of Mauritius gives a very remarkable example, possess
perfect machinery ? In Holland, Belgium, Russia,
Germany, the United States, Spain, the Cape, and
Australia, is the triumph of the principle we defend
the result of the employment of those particular
machines which are hardly known there, and which in
some localities have never been heard of ?

On the contrary, the white Sugar trade is not the
sole cause of improved machinery ; it is also more
especially that of the great mass of the consumers,
who have certainly a right to be represented, and
whose voice, like that of the chorus in ancient
tragedy, will always be heard by a Government resting
on universal suffrage, and having a proper care for
all that may contribute to raise the level of material
comfort. And how can such a Government accomplish
that result, or rather let us say that duty, which its
origin especially imposes on it, if it be not by giving
a free development, in conformity with their natural
tendencies, to all branches of production, whether
agricultural or manufacturing, and by making clearer
the source which is to supply a wide, pure stream
for future ages, from the innumerable accumulated
incumbrances of the past. And if we attach such
importance to the question of standards, it is precisely
because their suppression has brought Sugar industry so
decidedly forward in that fruitful path where producers
and consumers find a common interest, and which
is the characteristic of progress ; and because their

re-establishment would cause a re-action and intermi-
nable conflicts between the parties interested, a result
which it is impossible the Emperor could allow, or the
Sugar interests desire. Leave, then, the standards as
they are, and do not seek to resuscitate that vain form
of the past which has for the last three years met
with all it wanted, viz., oblivion.

X.

The law of May 23rd, 1860, by suppressing the
ancient mode of classification, by means of which those
duties were established, has given, as we have seen, a
decided advantage, in the French market, to the finest
Sugars, and allowed the refiners to obtain a better
per-centage. The decree of January 16th, 1861, by
suppressing the extra-duty of 3 francs on foreign
Sugars imported in French bottoms, has brought about
a very considerable importation of those kinds of
Sugars, and the decree of June 24th, 1861, admitting
the same Sugars imported in foreign bottoms to the
drawback, was of a nature to accomplish this end,
and to render our importation market one of the most
considerable in Europe. If the decrees, which we are
quoting, had for their object to lower the price of
Sugar in France, and at the same time to largely
develope refining for exportation, that object has
assuredly been attained even if not surpassed, and it

would obtain our entire approbation, if it were equally
profitable to all branches of the Sugar trade.

To form an idea of the magnitude of our imports
and exports of Sugar, in consequence of the measures
we have just quoted, we need only consult the
following statistics:—In 1860 there were imported
into France 60,496,812 kilos. of foreign Sugar; in
1861, 958,02,687 kilos.; in 1862, 129,167,132 kilos.
The importations, we see, have nearly doubled in the
course of last year. With regard to exportations of
refined Sugars, the same statistics supply us with the
following figures:—1860, 51,654,377 kilos.; 1861,
52,836,988 kilos.; 1862, 79,250,282 kilos.; this
last quantity, which, by calculating on the basis
of 120 kilos. of raw Sugar, to 100 kilos. of refined,
gives as a corresponding quantity 95,100,338 kilos.,
proves likewise that the two calculations are *not* just,
and that a great portion of foreign Sugar, so exten-
sively imported, remains in our warehouses to interfere
with our home consumption. In this respect the commercial position speaks more eloquently than we
could, and discloses more than all our reasonings.
With a home and colonial production, more than
sufficient for the national consumption, it remains
evident that the accumulation of foreign Sugars is a
cause of trouble, from which we must infer that there
is either too much importation or too little exportation, and that there is between both a want of equi-
librium which it is desirable to remedy.

Starting from this very simple idea, and without
taking into account the various elements which act so

important a part in the exportation, such as the extra-duty on foreign bottoms, the allowance to colonial Sugar, the per-centage, and, lastly, the alleged interests of the merchant navy, the beet-root Sugar-manufac-turers, forced to find a means of escape from the super-abundant amount on hand, and the gradual reduction of prices, have naturally asked why their beet Sugar should not be exported, and why this facility of free exchange, granted to similar foreign produce, should be refused to theirs, and thus establish a system of exceptions and privileges in direct op-position to the principles of free trade so greatly praised, and recently applied to every branch of manufactured productions except theirs ? A singular denial of justice truly, against which they have risen with all their might through their representatives. But these complaints were immediately drowned by the voices of those strange free traders at certain ports, who have invented a free trade of their own, and who now find that what is true at Nantes, Bor-deaux, Marseilles, and Havre, cannot be so at Lille, Douai, St. Quentin, or Valenciennes.

From this point of view it is impossible to find a single good argument against the exportation of refined home-made Sugar, which has the same claim to the drawback as colonial or foreign Sugar, which has not the exclusive privilege of the home market, and which, when that outlet is closed, should have the liberty to seek a better wherever it can. In what should the position of a Sugar produced in France be different from that of a Sugar produced in foreign parts ?

This is what we find impossible to comprehend. If free trade be applied in reality to all the products of the soil, why should Sugar form an exception ? If our corn, our wines, our oils, can now freely pass the frontiers of land and sea, home-made Sugar, which is an agricultural product of the first order, and which, as a manufactured commodity, represents the additional value of labour truly national, cannot, without great injustice and manifest infraction of the principles which form the basis of our commercial system, be legally prevented from choosing the most advantageous market. What ! the Sugar made in Cuba, Porto Rico, Brazil,—that Sugar which carries with it the stamp of slavery which is the disgrace as well as disturbance of half the New World,—shall it have power to land in our ports, and compete with our native Sugar ? Shall it be allowed to fill our warehouses, to remain within our walls, or pass our frontiers at pleasure, without our having the liberty to oppose its progress, or to contend with it on an equal footing ? For it is only equality we ask, and the complaints of our beet-root Sugar-manufacturers, we must frankly declare, go no further than claiming the exercise of its most legitimate right —that of disposing of its products wherever there be a buyer, an exchange, or a market.

"Sugar," they contend, "is an element of freight "which it is essential to preserve for our merchant " men ; the interest of the mercantile navy is opposed " to the exportation of refined home-made Sugar." Is that old argument, which we hear from every commission agent, of the real weight and value they attach to it? Is it really true that the admission of beet-root Sugar to the drawback would be the ruin of our mercantile navy? We may, at least, be allowed to question it, if we prove that foreign shipping is not at all interested in its transport. It is known that the Sugar of our colonies is used entirely for home consumption, and that foreign Sugars are the only ones re-exported. We have seen moreover that there has been imported into France, in 1862, 129,167,132 kilogrammes of foreign Sugar, 108,683,630 kilos. of which have paid duty. Of this last quantity the importations in French bottoms are 60,128,677 kilos., viz., 55 per cent. of the whole; and we have seen also that the re-exportation, under the denomination of refined, corresponded to 95,100,338 kilos. The proportion of 55 per cent. ascribed to French shipping, being taken as a basis, gives an amount of importation equal to 52,250 tons, or the freight of about 100 ships, middle tonnage, such as those which take freight in our colonies. Now, what has been the whole amount from our ports in 1862? 28,822 ships, and 4,566,673 tons, of which 12,374 ships and 1,907,897 tons belong to French shipping; so that this important element of freight, so highly prized in our ports, represents but 1·15 per cent. of the whole amount, and 2·75 per cent. of the entire French shipping. With these figures before their eyes, will they still say that the transport of foreign Sugar is indispensable to our mercantile navy, which would be ruined by the admission of home-grown Sugar to the drawback?

In order, then, to allow about 100 ships, manned by some 1,000 or 1,200 sailors, to navigate from India to Marseilles, or from the Mexican Gulf to Havre, they force a trade employing 40,000 or 50,000 hands, which is the foundation of the agricultural property in our most wealthy departments, to remain without the pale of common rights. You demand freight for your shipping; then why do you not take that which you leave to foreign bottoms, by which 58 per cent. of your carriage is effected? There would be more profit and more praise in this, than in cramping a trade which should never have been permitted to exist, if not allowed to grow. Its present production troubles you; its future, which is that of our agriculture, seems to make you uneasy, as if, in a well-organized society under the guidance of a good political economy, all interests did not tend to balance one another; as if all branches of agricultural and manufacturing productions were not equally free to expand.

The good example of England proves that the agricultural interest is not antagonistic to the shipping interest, and it is by no means proved that the development of the beet-root Sugar industry, great as it might be supposed, can interfere with our mercantile navy, whose progress, for the last twenty years, it has never interrupted. Is it not, then, evident that if there be more Sugar made in France, there will also be more corn and more meat, and that, in consequence of greater comfort among the population, the merchant service will find in an increase of trade some compensation for the item of freight which it considers so indispensable to its prosperity, notwithstanding its relative insignificance? Whatever be the real value of that argument concerning a reserved freight for our shipping, still it is certain that it cannot be upheld on principle, and that, in a system of perfect free trade, it could not be admitted without a manifest contradiction, against which the injured interest would never cease to protest as it does at the present day.

If you do not allow the native Sugar-manufacturer to export his products with allowance of drawback, do you think he would not justly demand the expulsion of foreign Sugar from the French market, which comes from all parts to enter into competition with him, and against which he cannot contend but with unequal arms? But that would be returning to a protective system, and the native Sugar-manufacturer knows that nations never retrace their footsteps, as rivers never return to their sources. He cordially accepts free trade, but he wants a real and sincere one, which can only be after the admission of his Sugar to the drawback which will open to him and to others the markets of Italy, Switzerland, Algeria, and the Levant, as well as those of the Black Sea, from which we have lately driven England, and even those of England itself, where beet-root Sugar will successfully contend with the Sugars from all the colonies and countries in the world. These markets belong to it as well as to the cane Sugars made in Cuba, Mauritius, or Brazil, and you have not even the shadow of a right to interdict them from it.

XI.

Certain countries among those we have just enume-
rated, viz., Italy, Switzerland, Turkey, do not manufacture Sugar ; others, such as Austria and Russia,
do not make enough for their own consumption ;
whilst others, like England, find it their interest,
for different commercial reasons, to import from the
European markets. The result of these conditions
is a vast international exchange of refined Sugars in
the various ports of the Atlantic and Mediterranean
Sea, unequally divided between the refiners of Holland,
France, England, and Belgium. Already, before the
revolution of 1793, French refiners exported their
produce to Italy, Switzerland, and Germany. That
commerce, interrupted during our political disturbances
and prolonged wars, was resumed at the Peace, and
became the object of various legislative measures, which
it would be too long to recount, but which never
had any other object than to favour the industry of
the refiners in France, and to procure freight for our
shipping. In order to attain this end, which agrees so
well with the protection long prevalent, the system of
primes (premiums on exportation) was invented, as
that of the graduated tariff had previously been, for in
fact one will not answer without the other, as is found
at the present time.

The drawback is often confounded with this premium, and yet they are two very different things : there may be a drawback without *prime*, for the true principle of the drawback is that which signifies the simple and clear return, neither more nor less, of the duty paid at the entrance on any merchandise allowed to be exported. Supposing I enter 100 kilos. of Sugar, which pay to the Customs 42 francs ; I export the said 100 kilos., and the Custom-house returns me 42 francs. This is an application of the principle, and would be very simple, if the Sugar was exported as it is imported ; but it comes in coarse, and goes out refined, and therefore has suffered a waste. What is that waste ? Here comes the question of per-centage. We know how much wheat loses by being reduced to flour ; or pig-iron into wrought-iron ; or iron to steel. How much, then, is lost by transforming 100 kilogrammes of raw into loaf Sugar ?

At the end of the seventeenth century, the refiners of Martinique took seven lbs. of brown to make one of white Sugar ; but we are far removed from that time, when the art was still in its infancy, and, not to lose our time in useless historical considerations, let us come at once to the modern per-centage, which we find fixed at 70, 75, and 76 per cent. ; that is to say, it has been successively admitted that 100 kilos. of raw Sugar yield in the refinery 70, 75, or 76 kilos. of white Sugar ; and hence the exportation of this quantity gives a claim to the return of the first duty paid on the quantity which produced it, viz., 42 francs, if the duty has been 42 francs. This appears very simple, but it is not so; for now, as it was from the first time of exportation, the percentage is a fiction, and the drawback a *prime* (premium on exportation).

We have already said that we know what wheat loses in being reduced to flour, pig-iron to wrought, iron to steel; but do we really know? Clearly not; for it is a question of progress, and of process. Do we know any better what one hundred weight of raw Sugar yields to the refiner? Certainly not. The per-centage is a result essentially variable, which depends on the origin of the Sugar, the improvements introduced in the first process, and the nature of that process. That per-centage is not now what it was ten years ago, five years ago, or even last year. You reckoned it lately at 70, then at 76, now at 80; what will it be to-morrow, and what is it in reality? We do not indeed think it will be possible to come to any certain understanding on this question, which cannot be settled by laws, and which the Legislature should resign if it does not desire unconsciously to continue to favour certain classes living corruptly at the expense of the Treasury. The percentage is a fiction, and will always be so; it will be either too low or too high, and in either case it will injure interests which we should neither protect nor oppress, and which have a right to expect from the Government—whose peculiar duty it is to distribute it to all—equity and justice.

Now, we ask, is there anything resembling the application of those two great principles in our present

system of exportation ? Let it be judged from the
following facts, which are only too well known, and
which we should not the less particularize for a complete understanding of the question, in order to bring
into broad light the contradictions and inconsequences
of certain parts of the actual legislation on Sugar.
We know that the legal per-centage is 76 per cent. A
similar amount of refined Sugar exported has a right,
on the presentation of the receipts, to the repayment
of duty paid on 100 kilos. of raw Sugar. But in
consequence of the return of the duty on colonial
Sugars, and the extra-tax on foreign ships, we know
that the duty is not the same on all Sugar. The
duty on Réunion Sugar is 34·80 ; on the West
Indian, 38·40 ; on home-made and foreign, 42 francs ;
to which last we must add, the extra-duty on
foreign ships, which in certain cases amounts to 44
and 45 francs. There are as many duties as drawbacks, and the higher the one so is it with the other.
Thus, by the scale of duties the drawback is 45·78
for Réunion Sugar ; 50·52 for West Indian ; 55·21
for foreign, in French bottoms ; 59·21 for Indian
foreign Sugar, in foreign bottoms, estimated upon
an 100 kilos. of refined Sugar.

What is the result of this in practice ? As the
only thing required of the exporter is proof of the pay-
ment of duty on the quantity of raw Sugar (which,
according to the legal per-centage, corresponds with the
quantity of refined Sugar exported,) viz., the receipt,
they refine with Sugar the least taxed, and they
export those which pay the highest duty ; and

this is another fiction to be added to that of the per-centage, since the foreign Sugar which supplies the receipt for the drawback is consumed, whilst colonial or home-made Sugar, intended for home consumption, is, in reality, exported. Hence abuses, and profits, which may be justly termed unlawful; hence the artificial introduction of foreign Sugars, principally in foreign bottoms, with no other object but to procure receipts, which, as we see, give rise to a most lucrative business, the profits of which, as in the fable of the lawyer and the oyster, are divided between the refiner and the importer, leaving to the exchequer nothing but the *shell.*

But the greatest inconvenience from this scandalous, though legal, traffic is to falsify the natural conditions of the market, by giving to foreign produce an advantage which they only owe to the receipts they carry with them, and thus exclude, from the export market, the Sugars less taxed, viz., those of our colonies. We find the official proof of it in the commercial and financial documents published by the Custom-house department, and in which we find that in 1860 the drawbacks on colonial Sugar were 12,526,850 francs, whilst in 1862 they were but 106 francs. On the other hand, the drawbacks on foreign Sugar, which in 1860 were only 20,350,171 francs, amounted to 38,649,804 francs for that same year 1862, in which our exportation trade was so greatly extended; and which the year 1863, owing to the same causes, again promises to surpass.

On the other hand, the refiner, in consequence of

E

the difference between the legal and real per-centage, which is known to equal 9 per cent., receives, at the expense of the treasury, as well as of the consumer, an advantage of 3 francs 50 cents or 4 francs, which, added to the profit made by the traffic in receipts, constitute for him a truly regal position on a market which he commands already by the amount of his capital, no less than by the fortunate result of speculations, unwittingly favoured by imperfect legislation. In sight of such manifest abuses, and of conditions so greatly in favour of a trade, in whose hands it may be said that " Sugar turns to gold," how can we be astonished at the extension of its monopoly and the rapid increase of its operations, of which we may judge by this fact, that we export at the present day more Sugar than Holland itself, that famous land of export refinery.

For instance, the exportation of Holland in refined Sugars for 1862 was only 63,731 tons, whilst that of France was 79,250 tons for the same year. Thus, then, our refiners have become greater than those of good, quiet Holland, and are in the way of becoming the purveyors of Europe, Asia, and part of America. They will soon be, nay, they are already, the first exporters of Sugar in the world. We ought surely to praise this result, so well calculated to excite the commercial ambition of a people who have large trading ports on both oceans ; but such a position is not taken by storm, and can only be obtained by patient efforts, and, above all, by the total absence of everything that resembles protection. Protection is, at the present

time, a bad means of ensuring the triumph of any
branch of industry soever ; it is a tradition of the
past, which we must repudiate, but to which the
exportation refiners in France are devotedly attached,
who, it cannot be denied, are highly protected by
a system of *primes*, hidden in a mechanism the com-
plication of which may appear innocent at first, but
which clever hands know admirably well how to work,
although they cannot hide the fallacy of its principle,
and their inability to create anything lasting.

In fact, this excessive development of the refining
industry in our ports is entirely artificial.* But were
it even more natural, we might justly inquire whether
it constitutes an interest of sufficient importance to
induce the Government to influence the Sugar question, and to prevent its rational solution, the first step
towards which would be equalization ? We do not

---

* The statistics of refined 'Sugars exported from 1827 to 1861 are
represented by the following figures, calculated on a mean per-centage of
70 per cent. for the first twenty years, and of 75 per cent. for the last fifteen.
We treat, as will be seen, of Raw Sugar :—

    1827 to 1836 ... ... 10,594,100 kilogrammes.
    1837 to 1846 ... ... 10,083,800 „
    1847 to 1856 ... ... 24,361,300 „
    1857 to 1861 ... ... 64,946,600 „

We have seen above that the exportation of refined Sugar for the last
three years had been as follows :—

    1860 ... ... 51,654,377 kilogrammes.
    1861 ... ... 52,836,938 „
    1862 ... ... 79,250,282 „

This last quantity, calculated on the actual per-centage of 76 per cent.,
represents in raw Sugar 104,276,690 kilos. ; it is enough to compare these
figures with those of the preceding years, to be convinced that we have good
ground for asserting that the export refining has increased in France beyond
all due proportion, and which can only proceed from the artificial encouragement it finds in the combinations of the Custom-house tariff, by which it
profits so largely,

think so ; and if the reader has kindly followed our explanations, he must see that the refining interest, and above all that interested in export refining, is the stumbling-block, and that this interest alone is an obstacle to measures that should be taken, and keeps in check numerous other branches interested in a question where it should act but a secondary part. For the whole cannot be subordinate to a part, and it is impossible, reasonably, to admit that the manufacture of Sugar, not only in France, but in our colonies, is to depend for a single instant on the conditions that a branch of it may wish to impose; an industry in which skilful speculation acts the chief part, but great only by its immense capital and large profits. Everything that is possible has been said on this subject, and what can we add to evidence which springs from such dissimilar sources and interests ?

It would be as absurd to attempt comparing the army of the King of Dahomey to that of a European sovereign, as to contrast a few thousand pale mechanics whom refiners employ in our sea-ports with those innumerable labourers occupied in extracting Sugar from the cane or beet-root. Other branches of trade cannot even be compared to it. Sugar is everything to the colonies : it is agriculture, trade, and commerce ; it is population, mercantile-marine, and credit ; it is a multifarious source of exchange ; it is even social life. In France, Sugar is the life of the rural population in our richest departments ; and whilst it is the nerve of a great number of additional trades, it constitutes an agricultural interest of the

highest order, which cannot be touched without wound-
ing public resources to the quick, and without giving
a terrible shock to the landed interest, and to agricultural and industrial produce.

If we contrast interests so important, and so worthy
of consideration, with that of export refining, which
is, as we have seen, the stumbling-block, what do
we find? about one hundred ships navigating, and
a freight of some 50,000 tons to be divided among a
few ship-owners, and fifteen or twenty refiners already
receiving undue profits by means of the drawback;
and it is for this that people puzzle themselves with
questions of per-centage, that they talk of re-establishing the standards, that they again question everything,
that they want to revive restrictions, abuses, privileges which are the negation of commercial liberty,
and which nullify a part of the political programme of
the Emperor.

However, that must not be; and if a solution is at
length to be obtained, it must be given on the side of
reason, of justice, and of the most absolute equality
for all interests engaged in the question, among which
those of the first importance are our great Sugar
trade, both native and colonial.

We have all heard of that African tree, the shade of which is fatal to all living beings who have the misfortune to linger beneath it. Beneath its shade is death; a little farther, beyond the reach of its branches, are light, life, and liberty. The privileged interests we have just considered may be compared to this tree. If we remain under their deadly influence, we must relinquish all hope. If we escape, our ideas are enlarged, and facts appear in their true light. Let, then, the Sugar question no longer be confined to the narrow circle of such and such an interest; let it be no longer tossed from one hand to the other, like the ball to which we have compared it; let it at last enter into the inflexible rule of those principles which alone can serve as a criterion upon which to form our judgment.

Now, what are those principles which also represent interests, but interests that we are proud to defend, and that every one is bound to support against the obstacles to which they are naturally exposed? They are the interests of the consumers, of progress, of the exchequer, and of trade in general. The interest of the consumer, to which we purposely give precedence, seems, indeed, to be the one the least thought of, as if Sugar were not made for those who use it;

as if bread, for example, interested the millers and bakers more than the mass of the people who consume it. What do the thirty-eight millions of Sugar-eaters whom we count in France demand of the few hundred manufacturers who supply it, if it be not that this commodity should be good, plentiful, and cheap? But how to satisfy so legitimate a desire with those restrictive laws which we have inherited from our fathers, and which "the Tories," with regard to the Sugar question, wish to revive? Is it by re-establishing the standards, for instance, that you will make cheap Sugar? And how will you effect it with a system which repudiates science, and which no disinterested manufacturer would care to support?

The argument of an abundant freight for our shipping was for a long time the *cheval-de bataille* of the partisans of the scale, who, it will be readily supposed, were ship-owners, supported more or less by the refiners, a sort of hybrid to be met with in a few of our ports, and who, according to custom, continue to hold the same argument. It might be a very innocent game, if there were not very grave interests at stake, which are thus kept suspended, and prevented from acquiring their natural development. "What will become of our navy if they export white Sugar? What will become of our refiners if they import no more raw Sugar?" Has not this been your language for the last two centuries, and do you suppose, Burgraves of the Sugar question, that it is still right, and that you can retain your prejudices, defying the progress of time, and

disarming truth itself ? You desire freight for the navy !
We would give you some, but not as in England,
where, owing to the graduated tariff, they are still
reduced to the construction of special ships in order to
save the Molasses which, during the voyage, drains
from the bad Sugars which she compels her colonies to
manufacture, and which otherwise would have to be
thrown overboard, a thing which is frequently done.*
We want to give you freight, but it shall be a freight
of white, pure Sugar, which by its abundance shall
render your ships insufficient, and will force you to
double the number of your vessels and sailors.

Twenty years past, when M. Peligot made that
remarkable Report to the Minister of Marine,† which
was as a ray of light on the situation of our colonial
trade, they learned, with a surprise easy to be understood, that the cane, which contains theoretically 18
per cent. of crystallized Sugar, yielded in practice
only 5 per cent., and that the colonial trade was still
at the per-centage of the time of Father Labat,‡ who
lived two centuries ago. Science profited by that
exposure, and there are now at Guadaloupe and Martinique a great number of central factories which
guarantee to the planter this 5 per cent. for the price
of their canes, and extract on their side 10 per cent., obtained by the happy division between agricultural and
manufacturing labour, by the employment of the best

---

* "Report from the Select Committee on Sugar Duties."
† Report to Admiral Duperré, 1842. See also Governor Barkly's Re-
port, p. 71.
‡ See Note, p. 69.

machinery, and on condition that it be pure, white, and fit for immediate consumption. You may see specimens of it at Nantes, and in all our sea-ports, and this is the best argument we can adduce in favour of so marked a progress.

We appeal to the authority of our most illustrious scientific men, such as Dumas, Payen, Peligot, and all those who have given their time to the triumph of progress and science, and we ask them if it is not true that modern industry has extracted out of nothing this additional quantity of 5 per cent., which we want to ensure both to our shipping interests and our own consumption, and which you repel in the name of something we know not what. Let a legislation, having only in view the general good, allow such white Sugar to be made; let 10 per cent. be obtained, and 60 millions of kilos., the production of our West Indian colonies, will rise to 120 millions. That is an increase of freight of more than 60,000 tons, which could never exist with the standards, for we cannot repeat it too often, and it is an axiom to which we would call the special attention of all who are strangers to the manufacture of Sugar, —*The whiter and purer, the more Sugar is made.*

We no longer belong to the time when white Sugar could only be obtained by mechanical means, by filtering with water, or with clear syrup, by "claying," or any other empirical process, such as dissolving a portion of the Sugar in order to whiten the rest. Such means are no longer employed, and we are speaking here of the colonial as well as home manufacture, where the chief art of making white Sugar consists solely in the employment of chemical means which tend to separate and to detach the Sugar which *nature makes white,* and which all efforts must be made to extract as such. Now, who can say that we have not succeeded ? " Let facts speak for themselves," said an illustrious writer.* This they do, for they answer with forty-three home and colonial manufactories, created during the last three years under an enlightened legislation. They reply with 41 million kilos. of superior Sugar, fit for consumption, or in the best state for refining. They reply with an improved means of production, which represents already a sixth part of our consumption. Within ten years, or possibly less, the whole colonial and home production would be transformed ; within ten years, and the French market—that market of 40 millions of consumers — would be wholly supplied with white Sugars fit for immediate consumption, or those most economical for refining. And it is this gigantic progress, which might be the pride of our legislation and our trade, that you would smother in its origin for the benefit of a few miserable private interests. This is, indeed, the grain of sand which stops the working of the whole machinery ; it is like the stone which throws the locomotive off the rails. But a danger foreseen is less to be dreaded, and the prudence of Government, we trust, will preserve us from this.

* Louis Napoleon Bonaparte.

To state results such as these, to express hopes already confirmed by the experience of past years, is almost conclusive ; and how else can we remain firm to our principles, which force us to regard the solution in its most simple form. What does the consumer require ?—White, pure, cheap Sugar ; but this is the interest of the Exchequer, which will receive more in proportion as more is used. On this basis all the great interests agree, and if we have justly condemned a legislation, which maintained a fiscal distinction between raw and white Sugar at a time when the manufacture was still in its infancy, with how much greater reason must we do it now, and demand that powdered Sugar, loaf Sugar, and that Sugar which is evidently the product of the first manufacture, should not be treated worse than the old white Sugar, which, in comparison with the present magnificent productions, is little more than fine raw Sugar. What, because by means of my capital, my exertions, my industry, and my ability, I have made Sugar fit to enter the market in competition with refined Sugar, will you impose on me an extra-tax, and burden my productions with a heavier duty ? That would be unjust, as it would only benefit one class accustomed by tradition to live by its privileges ; for it is evident that the refiner alone would have to fear the fixed tax we propose, and which we demand as the only solution of the Sugar question.

We must now end this question, which for the last twenty years has been like a night-mare to our politicians, who, in their perplexity, must have said many

times : " What can be done regarding the Sugar ques-
" tion ? " Where should we be, if every subject of
political economy were in as complicated a state ?
The whole lives of our statesmen would not suffice
to unravel such confusion. Is there a Tea, Coffee,
Wine, or Spirit question ? Does not Tea pay the same
duty, let it be green or black, let it be of a superior
or inferior quality ?* Does not Coffee, whether from
Mocha, Padang, India, or Brazil, pay the same duty ?
Does not Wine, whether from Burgundy or Medoc,
pay the same duty, or is it taxed according to its
colour, flavour, or quality ?† Does not alcohol,
whether from corn, Molasses, or beet-root, pay the
same duty ? Does not the law allow me to manufacture as I choose that alcohol which originally
comes from pure Sugar, to make with it brandy or
spirit at 95 degrees, to sell it simple or rectified ?
What would people think of a law imposing a
higher duty on pure alcohol made in the distilleries
than on those from the rectifiers ? Yet such is the
case in relation to Sugar, since the one made in
a manufactory, and which can arrive at the highest
perfection, that is to say, deserve the burthensome
title of " *assimilated to refined*," is subjected
to an extra-tax of one-tenth, which the refiners can

---

* There were in England differential duties on Teas. Under that system
there was a vast importation of inferior qualities—*Bohea Teas*. Since the
equalization of duties, only good Teas are consumed.—("Report on Sugar
Duties," page 113.)

† It must be remembered the writer is speaking of France, and that
his remarks on wine do not apply to us.—ED.

avoid.* Let them be taxed also if you like; that will suit us as well, for it agrees with our theory of equalizing the tax on all Sugars, which is our great object, and which, we repeat, is the only means of solving the Sugar question in the interest of the consumer, the producer, and the Treasury.

By this system everything becomes logical and simple, and the law for Sugar may be defined in a few words. None of the most important interests which we have mentioned are injured, nor are the secondary ones either. It is quite clear that if the independent refiners wished to contend with the refiners of beet-root Sugar with any chance of success, they could only do so by giving more and more encouragement to raw Sugar of the highest value, which would simply be a larger extension of the advantages our manufactures have derived for the last three years from the suppression of the standards. Every one would then make better, richer, and purer Sugar,

---

* If, starting from this fact, that all Sugars employed by the refiners pay only the duty on raw Sugar, which is at present 42 francs, whilst white Sugars from home manufactories, either crushed or in loaf, pay an extra-tax of one-tenth, say, 46 francs 20 cents., we arrive at the conclusion that the extra-tax on refined is nothing less than a protection for the refining interest. The Exchequer in reality does not benefit by this difference, which is only profitable to the refining-pan. For without that extra-tax, which has no other effect but the re-melting of a quantity of Sugar, without use for any one except the forty or fifty artisans who perform that operation, and which they strive to connect with the great principle of the division of labour, they would make in a few years in our beet-manufactories as much white as they make raw Sugar at the present day. Who, then, does not see that the consumer would have the benefit of a reduction of price equal to the extra-tax, and that the Exchequer, on the other side, in consequence of a larger consumption, would have a certain increase of revenue ? It is important to bear in mind, that everything is untrue which is contrary to principle.

in order to diminish as much as possible the refiners'
waste, and that he might work with the smallest margin,
which, as we have seen, was 90 francs but thirty years
ago, and is now only 25 or even 20 francs ; and this,
owing to the improvement in machinery, and favoured
by a liberal legislation, such as we now demand, may fall
to 8 or 10 francs, the true representation of a fancy
price, and the exact difference that should exist
between loaf Sugar and pure white Sugar in powder.
We have already said that we desire an union of interests, not opposition ; and it cannot be admitted that
the refining interest, which is so strong and powerful,
can be so easily destroyed. There is but one duty in
Australia, and yet they have refining establishments ;
but they use the finest Sugars of Mauritius and
India, whilst the English only use the dregs ; that is
all the difference.

We therefore ask for a single duty on all
Sugars, whether crushed or loaf, whether refined
or not. There remains, it is true, the question of
exportation, an interest which we must take into
account, although we have made the best of their faults.
We have, in a preceding chapter, expressed our repug-
nance to a fixed per-centage, and proved how difficult
it was to emerge from the fictions it engenders. We
begin, therefore, by inquiring whether it be expe-
dient to return to ancient data, and to introduce again
into the law an element of so variable a nature, and
which will have to be revised every year. Let it be
raised to 80 per cent., and what certainty have you
that it will not be ere long at 85, soon after at

90, and later again at 95 per cent. ? For our own part, we are of opinion that nothing stable can be founded on this truly disturbing element of the Sugar question, which has not, and never should have, the importance ascribed to it, and without which everything would become easy. When we think of what takes place in the metal trade, where the same quantity imported, be it cast or pig-iron, must be represented in the quantity exported, in whatever manner it may have been worked, we naturally ask, whether this is not the indication of an equitable and rational solution ; and if we should not at once cut short these drawbacks and per-centages, in calling the export refiner to export simply an equal quantity of Sugar to the one he has already brought in ? We do not see any other solution ; and if we consider that the manufacturers, who work in metals, have petitioned under every Government for a per-centage, which has justly been refused to them, saying, "You would deceive us in " your waste, which we should never be able to know ; " submit to the consequences of that waste, which are one "of the conditions of your manufacture, and look for a " compensation to that loss in your price of the manufac- "tured material," we ask if the same language should not be held to the refiners ; and if, with the certain improvement in manufacture, the system of weight for weight is not the most equitable, and the most simple; and if, in a word, its application would not alone have the power at once to reform all the abuses, which, even with a higher per-centage, will never cease to exist, and which, in placing the Sugar question in a

false light, will always prevent that rational solution
at which, nevertheless, we must arrive.*

It only remains for us to examine whether there be
any occasion to maintain *provisionally*, that is to say,
until the expiration of the delay granted by the Legislature, the reduction of the tax on colonial Sugars.†
This is a question concerning which the colonies ought
first to be consulted ; nevertheless, considering the
peculiar situation of those countries, and their obligation to provide for the necessary number of hands

---

* We do not object to the employment of all means compatible with our
new commercial regulations, in order to encourage the extension of export
refining in France, on condition, however, that the position in which it
shall be placed shall no longer disturb much higher interests. The interests of the export refiners, distinct from those of the ship-owners, which
we have appreciated at their just value, are nothing more, in reality, than the
interests of the hands they employ ; they are expressed by the figures of
2 francs 50 cents, or 3 francs, per 100 kilos. of refined Sugar, which, for a
quantity of 80,000 tons exported in 1862, give a sum total of 2,400,000 francs,
at the highest estimate. As to the *prime d'exportation* (export encouragement, not drawback) represented by the Sugar unredeemed, and absorbed in
consumption, it is at the present 6,300,000 francs, and might be considerably
increased, if the per-centage increase, as there is no doubt it will. Government, with the present system of-drawback, can never know what it is
giving to a trade which thinks it cannot exist without immunities and privileges ; but if it were true that it could not exist without them, we ought at
least to know what it is we are allowing it, and to make a fixed grant, of which
the sole purpose would be to assist that branch of national labour which it represents, and which is, as stated above, from 2 francs 50 cents to 3 francs per
100 kilos. We could, then, if this system of weight for weight, which we
are advocating, appears too absolute or premature, adopt a temporary
arrangement, so that the sum granted to a national work should be added to
the duty returned, and would then constitute a fixed *prime* on all refined
Sugars exported, say, for instance, 44 or 45 francs, if the Sugar duty be 42
francs per 100 kilos. It would only be necessary afterwards to come to an
understanding with other nations for the adoption of a system which,
in our eyes, would spare existing interests without endangering sound
principles.

† Three francs until June 30th, 1866,—this is exclusively for Réunion ;
three francs more until June 30th, 1864 ; and only 1 franc 50 cents, from
that time to June 30th, 1865,

by continual and costly immigration, it seems to us but just to maintain that reduced tax until the expiration of the delay specified. With what relates to the extra-tax on foreign ships, considering that this is added to the duty on Sugar, there can be no doubt about suppressing it. Tax the foreign ships if advisable, but not the Sugar, for we do not want a higher duty on foreign any more than on colonial or beet-root Sugar. The principle on which we act does not admit of two weights and two measures, but we earnestly demand an absolute equality according to law for all Sugars.

What can be more simple than this law if we remain but true to our first principles? These may be summed up in a few words:—

A single uniform duty on all Sugars, whether coarse or refined, loaf or crushed.

The maintenance of the colonial reduced duties until the expiration of the delay granted by the law of May 23rd, 1860.

The repayment of duties for exportation on the basis of weight for weight.

The admission of all Sugars to the drawback, whether of colonial, foreign, or native production, whether imported in French or foreign bottoms.

The extension of the faculty of *abonnement.**

---

* The beet-root Sugar-manufacturer does not benefit as much as he would wish by the right of compounding which was granted by the law of May 23rd, 1860, and that for many reasons. First, the *tax de la prise en charge* (rate), fixed at 1,425 grs., is too high not to give him in most places a fear of suffering from deficiencies which he would have to bear. Secondly, the rate, whatever it is, should be calculated upon a previous trial of three years at

Thus, the principles which should guide us in the reform (now acknowledged unavoidable) of the laws respecting Sugar are those of the most absolute liberty. They are the principles dictated by the Emperor in his letter of January 5th, 1860, and form the basis of that programme of political economy which our commerce and trade accepted as the signal of a new æra as promising as it was unexpected.

As, in concluding this essay, I have again alluded to the name of the chief of the State, let me be allowed to raise my feeble voice, and say to him, " Sire, the " Sugar interest, that vast industry, the subject of so " enlightened, so profound a solicitude on your part, " demands unity, strength, and stability, and expects " from you the *initiative* of one of those extensive " reforms which is in keeping with your character, and " which marks a notable epoch and a glorious reign."

---

least, which would allow the manufacturer to introduce in his machinery any amelioration by the favour of this faculty. Thirdly, the obligation of paying the tax in advance, on the basis given by the defecation, constitutes a disadvantageous engagement if the Sugar remains, as often happens, in the warehouse for any length of time. On this last point, it is to be wished. that the ministerial decree of March 25th, 1863, which allows the duties on all Sugars warehoused to be paid on their being removed, though not later than the 31st July, 1863, should become the foundation of a distinct law.

Such are the principal modifications to be made to the *abonnement*, which, on these new conditions, would operate to the complete satisfaction of all the beet-root Sugar-manufacturers.

In France the tax on cane Sugar is collected at the frontier by
the Custom-house officers ; it is clear that the tax on home-made
Sugar cannot be raised otherwise than by means of the Excise. In
order to ensure the collection of so profitable a tax, which during
the last season did not amount to less than 72 million francs,
the French Government has subjected the manufacture of beet-
root Sugars to the most rigorous system of taxation, viz., by
fixing excisemen permanently in their establishments, where
they live day and night, and have their own private offices, with
fire and light provided by the manufacturers, deducting a
small allowance, and from which place they watch and follow
the whole process, and see that not a particle of Sugar escapes
the duty.

The energy displayed by such agents so situated must give
rise to extreme unpopularity, and it was to get rid of this
vexatious interference that the *abonnement* was proposed and
adopted by the law of May 23rd, 1860.

By the ordinary system of the Excise, the manufacturer is
taxed at the rate of 1,400 grammes of Sugar per degree
of density for each hectolitre of beet-root juice obtained and
proved at the defecation. This is the first element in esti-
mating the quantity of Sugar which the manufacturer may
afterwards obtain, and it seldom happens that this per-centage
is exact. There is consequently either a surplus or a deficiency ; in other words, the final result is either above or below
the first valuation, based on 1,400 grammes. In the first
case, the manufacturer pays for the surplus ; formerly, he
paid for the deficiency, viz., for the Sugar which had not
been obtained, which had remained a non-entity, and whose
existence had only been presumptive, the result of a calculation
necessarily empirical and imperfect ; for it must not be for-
gotten that there exists no practical means of ascertaining in
advance the manufactured per-centage of a liquor, and that the
legal basis of 1,400 is only an approximate figure.

An imperial decree of January the 7th, 1860, exempted the manufacturer from the iniquitous obligation of paying for deficiencies, but he has still to pay for the surplus. To avoid this necessity, and also to facilitate the transactions of the Excise, by establishing the tax on a fixed basis, which is previously known, the *abonnement* was proposed, which is nothing but a contract with the administration, by which the parties bind themselves to accept the chances, good or bad, of a new mode of taxation, the basis of which is fixed and determined each year before the beginning of the season by a decree published in the *Moniteur* or the *Bulletin des Lois*. That basis was fixed at 1,425 grammes, or 25 grammes more than according to the ordinary mode of Excise. Under these conditions, whether the manufacturer has a surplus or a deficiency, the Excise has no business to look into it. Besides, he has his full liberty, and makes grey, brown, or white Sugar, coarse or refined, without any disputes respecting their different values; in a word, he is completely free to manufacture just as he pleases.

Such is the *abonnement* which accomplished an undoubted improvement in the history of French legislation, but which the advocates of a graduated tax have caused to be suppressed in the projected law. During this very year, 61 manufacturers out of 368 have adopted the *abonnement*, and the former mode of Excise, so troublesome, so strict, and so hostile to progress, was fast disappearing. The extent of the re-action which is preparing shows how just was our defence of the *abonnement*, which was a powerful means of arriving at a cheap production, and which for that very reason the re-actionists will not have.

Note on the allusion to the Army of Coblentz, and M. Victorien Sardou.—Page 11.

ON the 29th of October, 1862, a comedy in four acts, by M. Victorien Sardou was represented, for the first time in Paris, at the Gymnasium, under the title of *Les Ganaches*, in which the author represented several characters of the old school supposed to be living in a corner of Brittany; a curious revival of times long gone by, amongst whom were a Marquis and a

Duke, who advocate the most retrograde opinions with respect
to their time, showing themselves sworn enemies of all refor-
mation, and all progress, and manifesting for railroads, in particular, an antipathy which eventually becomes nearly fatal to
both. The epithet of " Ganaches," which Mr. Sardou applies
to them, describes people that are old-fashioned, worn-out, and
out of date, who, unable to accustom themselves to the ideas
of the present day, oppose them on all occasions. This comedy
obtained a great success in France, where, for a short time,
the epithet of " Ganache " was universally applied to all who
were opposed to the ideas of progress entertained by the enlightened and energetic part of the French nation.

There is, consequently, between the " Ganache " of Mr. Sardou
and the famous army of Coblentz, which, during our first
revolution, recruited at that foreign frontier town among the
débris of the old French society, a similitude to which the
author makes allusion by the word *Ganache*. Though not
openly expressed, it is sufficiently understood from the description as thoroughly applicable to the supporters of the old
regulations on Sugar in France, viz., to the antiquated
defenders of the system of placing extra taxes upon colour
and quality.

Note on Father Labat.—Page 12.

Father Labat was the author of " *A Voyage to the American
Islands*," undertaken A.D. 1696. That was published shortly
afterwards, and contained some interesting details of the natural
history, manners, religion, and government of the people of
those countries. It contains also the history of wars, and other
events which happened during the stay of the author in that
region.

Father Labat belonged to the order of Dominicans, who
founded an establishment in Martinique, which the reverend
father, as chief of the mission, directed, and in which he gave
proof of great practical knowledge and extensive information.

Whether as planter, carpenter, mason, engineer, or refiner,
no art was foreign to him. One volume of his work is entirely
devoted to the description and consideration of the cultivation

and manufacture of Sugar, both of which he was the means of greatly improving.

The old-fashioned "batterie" or machines, i. e., the various pans for evaporation and boiling, were modified by him, and still bear his name. The same system is even now in use on the greater part of the Sugar plantations in Martinique and Guadaloupe.

The name of Father Labat was synonymous with progress a century and a half back; at the present time it means *routine.* The allusion made to a name, which once played an important historical part in the annals of our two little Sugar islands, refers to the employment of processes which had their merit at the time, though they now, after a lapse of nearly two centuries, have none, but on the contrary bring those who persist in using them to certain ruin.

Frequent allusions are made to the name of Father Labat in all discussions in France on the Sugar question, and this explanation will render them more intelligible to the English reader.

Note.—Page 19.

Extract from a Despatch from Governor Barkly to the Duke of Newcastle, dated British Guiana, 10th November, 1852. (No. 178.)

" Apparatus for carrying the manufacture of Sugar to a higher stage were likewise adopted here earlier than in any tropical country, the vacuum pan having, as mentioned by Mr. Austin, been put up on several estates twenty years ago, and though the diminished means and credit of the planters, and still more the discrimination according to quality enacted by the laws regulating the duties in Great Britain, have tended to discourage 'its extended use, both the plan of boiling in vacuo, and Gadesden's for boiling at a lower temperature than the ordinary, are spreading, the former being already practised on twenty-two plantations, and pans in course of erection on three others ; the latter already being in trial on three, whilst within my own knowledge either one or other improvement is contemplated by the proprietors of eight other estates. Were the grades of discriminating duty abandoned in regard to Sugars, 'equal to white clayed' and 'refined,' and one rate charged upon Sugar without reference to its fineness, I have no doubt indeed the vacuum pan would become universal on such estates as make 500 hogsheads and upwards, and Gadesden's pans, combined with centrifugals (or possibly the new apparatus of Rillieux, if found to answer, in an experiment about to be made here, as well as it is said to do in the United States), as requiring less outlay of capital on the smaller estates.

"Besides getting a larger return of superior Sugar from a given quantity of cane juice than they now do of the inferior quality, the planters would, by such means, save the large per-centage now lost from the drainage of their Muscovado Sugar on the voyage home, usually reckoned at more than a tenth.*

"The discouragement which the existing arrangement of duties offers to an improved system of manufacture will be best conceived from the following facts; first, that the process of 'spoiling' Sugar, when it seems better than would be likely to pass the lowest standard, is not of unfrequent occurrence on estates where the vacuum pan is used; second, that a gentleman in charge of an estate on which vast expense has been incurred for steam clarifiers, bag and charcoal filters, vacuum pans, and pneumatic pumps, assured me that for a further trifling outlay of about £100, he could, were it not for the quasi-prohibitive duty, ship the whole of his crop (1,000 tons) of a quality equal to refined Sugar, though made bonâ fide by a single process from the raw material.

"I venture most respectfully to conclude the observations which I have felt it my duty to make on a subject of so much importance to this colony, in the words of a report addressed by the celebrated chemist Peligot to the French Colonial Minister, in 1842 : 'If colourless Sugar cannot be produced from the cane (as was supposed a few years ago) ; if the Molasses, which impregnates and colours this Sugar cannot be removed ; if the production of colonial brown Sugar must remain station-ary as to quantity ; if the quality cannot be improved ; the

---

* 15 per cent., according to a late writer, vide " Facts and Observations," by Mr. A. Archbold.

excess of duty upon white Sugar may, to a certain extent, be comprehended and justified. But if, on the contrary, this colouration is the consequence of a bad mode of working ; if it be demonstrated that the Sugar which pre-exists in the cane is white ; that it is obtained white when a part is not destroyed ; that the proportion extracted is consequently as much greater as it is less coloured, what must be thought of a legislative measure which imposes upon that industry the exorbitant obligation of making small and bad products, and which places a barrier before one of the things which the law should most respect—improvement ?'

Exportation of Sugar from Mauritius to different places from the Crop 1843-44 to the Crop 1862-63.—Page 26.

Crops.	United Kingdom.	France.	Australian Colonies.	Cape.	Other Places.	TOTAL.
	Tons.	Tons.	Tons.	Tons.	Tons.	Tons.
1843-44	25,420	,,	95	1,058	9	26,582
1844-45	32,657	,,	1,649	572	16	34,894
1845-46	42,338	,,	1,826	1,436	10	45,610
1846-47	55,764	,,	1,722	1,922	150	59,558
1847-48	46,283	,,	4,606	3,826	118	54,833
1848-49	41,944	,,	3,312	2,180	6	47,442
1849-50	47,927	,,	2,871	2,783	224	53,805
1850-51	47,562	,,	2,454	1,899	355	52,270
1851-52	51,276	,,	4,139	5,848	65	61,328
1852-53	61,436	,,	7,245	3,302	38	72,021
1853-54	77,327	156	10,264	2,606	393	90,746
1854-55	68,592	11,624	11,830	5.038	1,357	98,441
1855-56	79,543	7,530	12,895	2,537	151	102,716
1856-57	56,041	21,662	16,826	3,250	1,539	99,318
1857-58	52,186	15,329	21,997	5,254	2,591	97,357
1858-59	59,471	18,725	21,242	4,742	2,025	106,205
1859-60	48,321	26,743	19,532	4,509	2,210	101,815
1860-61	82,845	12,232	19,220	4,134	2,997	121,428
1861-62	26,928	22,343	30,004	5,730	3,396	98,401
1862-63	76,209	31,213	31,829	6,168	9,210	141,215

Note.—Page 31.

From 1844 to 1854 English consumption increased from 17 lbs. per head per annum to 34 lbs., having barely averaged 17 lbs. since the year 1801.

After 1854, when it had reached 34 lbs. per head, this increase stopped, consumption receding to 30 and 28, and is now only 34 lbs. again.

It was in 1844 that differential taxation (differential as to country) was first partially abandoned.

In 1848, Government went still further, and provided for a gradual abandonment of the differential system as affected quality—measures that were followed by the extraordinary results narrated.

It was in 1854 that the Government, in the face of these facts, more widely extended the distinctive rates on Sugar.

It was from 1844 to 1854, a period of ten years, that the increase we have pointed out took place. During the first half of this period the reduction in the average tax was 12s. 1d., the increase per head 7 lbs.

From 1849 to 1854, the reduction being only 1s. 8d., a further increase was 10 lbs. more. Of the first period no one can doubt that a great portion of the increase was due, not so much to the fact of a reduction in duty, as to the vastly increased power of supply, to the permission to buy other Sugars besides those of one or two British possessions ; was due, in fact, to getting rid of one portion of our differential system.

But the increase from 1849 of 10 lbs. cannot be attributed to anything but the gradual assimilation of the duties ! And it is highly significant of this that in 1854, in spite of an average duty that was 6d. more than in 1853, the consumption sprung up that year alone 4 lbs. per head, whilst the price of Sugar to he consumer was absolutely 3s. 1d. less.

M S. Rickerby, Printer, Bell Court, 4a, Walbrook. E.C.

www.ingramcontent.com/pod-product-compliance
Lightning Source LLC
Chambersburg PA
CBHW021529270326
41930CB00008B/1168